# Time for Tea

## in Alberta

## A Tea House Guide

*Enjoy!*

### By
### MELANIE MONAI
### &
### JOAN PATTEN

*Melanie Monai*

*Joan Patten*

Pictured on front cover

**The Pic-A-Lilli Tea House**
**Holden, Alberta**

*Time for Tea in Alberta*
by
Melanie Monai & Joan Patten

First Printing — May 1996

**Copyright © 1996 by
Time for Tea Publishing**
Box 77014
Grandin Park Post Office
St. Albert, Alberta
Canada   T8N 6C1

All rights reserved. Except for reviews, no part of this book may be reproduced without permission from the publisher.

**Canadian Cataloguing in Publication Data**

Monai, Melanie, 1962 –

   Time for tea in Alberta: a tea house guide

   ISBN 1-895292-79-4

1.  Restaurants – Alberta – Guidebooks.   2. Afternoon teas – Alberta.   I. Patten, Joan, 1934-
II.  Title.

TX907.5.C22A43   1996 647.957123  C96-920045-5

Designed, Printed and Produced in Canada by:
Centax Books, a Division of PrintWest Communications Ltd.
Publishing Director: Margo Embury
1150 Eighth Avenue, Regina, Saskatchewan, Canada  S4R 1C9
(306) 525-2304   FAX: (306) 757-2439

2

# INTRODUCTION

This book was born, very appropriately, while we were having afternoon tea at a nearby tea house. We thought it might be fun to go to other places where afternoon tea is served and then write a guide book. We were right! Our research has been most enjoyable!

Phoning ahead sometimes saved a needless trip as some tea rooms are only open at certain times on certain days of the week. Making advance reservations ensured that everything was waiting for us when we arrived and that every item was fresh. Afternoon tea is about taking time to relax, socialize and browse, as well as drinking in the atmosphere. We became experts at this!

But then the unexpected happened! We heard of many other tea rooms which did not serve a traditional afternoon tea but were rich in history and character. Some are located in very interesting and unusual historic buildings and sites which give special glimpses and intriguing insights into Alberta's past. There are tea rooms in a former convent, school, railway station, post office, North West Mounted Police barracks, barn, and grain elevator, as well as in homes built many decades ago. No two places are alike, and each is unique in its own particular way. They have been restored and refurbished in varying degrees and have been brought back to life and continue to serve their communities. We decided to expand the book and include them too!

Without exception, we were met by friendly proprietors and/or managers who add a personal welcoming touch to their establishments. A keen eye to detail has made each of these interesting tea rooms an experience to remember. We also met other tea house patrons and swapped the names of places we had visited.

Last, but by no means least, we have enjoyed travelling the Alberta countryside seeing rolling farmlands, deep valleys with rivers, wetlands and wildlife, especially coyotes! We visited well-kept farms, various museums, villages, and small and large towns. Above them all was the constantly changing big sky of Alberta, sometimes an intense, cloudless blue, sometimes with marvellous cloud formations and, once, shrouded with the blackest clouds we have ever seen!

Perhaps you will be encouraged, as we were, to travel to places you have never visited before. Get out the map, get in the car, and go! You will meet a lot of friendly people and will have some lovely surprises. It has been a lot of fun for us, and we hope that it is for you, too.

# ACKNOWLEDGEMENTS

A special thank you to Sylvia, who suggested the name for our book, *Time For Tea.*

We are grateful to those who shared in our research for this book, especially John, Derry, Rose, Gastone, Natalie, Rachel, Christina, Catherine, Marita, Heather, and Margaret, and all those who have encouraged us.

We are also grateful to all of the proprietors and managers who so willingly shared with us the details, histories and, in some cases, photographs or drawings of their tea rooms. Many also suggested other tea rooms for us to contact, and we are particularly grateful to Violetta Link and Lorene Frere in this respect.

To the best of our knowledge, all information in this book is correct at the time of going to press. However, we suggest a phone call to the tea houses to confirm hours of operation and thus advoid possible disappointment.

*Melanie Monai and Joan Patten*

# THE AFTERNOON TEA TRADITION

*There are few hours in life more agreeable than the hour dedicated to the ceremony known as afternoon tea.*

*Henry James*

Anna, the seventh Duchess of Bedford, is believed to have introduced what would later become the tradition of afternoon tea. Finding she had "a sinking feeling" midway between luncheon and dinner, she began having tea and cakes in the afternoon with her friends.

Sandwiches, a traditional element of afternoon tea, were introduced earlier by John Montagu, the 4th Earl of Sandwich. He asked that his food be brought to him, as he was unable to pull himself away from the gaming table to the dining table. The food was placed between two slices of bread – hence sandwiches.

Initially, tea was very expensive, something only the wealthy could afford. However, Queen Victoria continued the afternoon break, which soon became a national tradition.

Traditional afternoon tea may include some or all of the following:

- finger sandwiches, savouries, scones with cream and preserves, cakes, biscuits (cookies), fruit or a fruit cup (a refreshing addition)
- tea, scones, jam and clotted cream (often a very acceptable and sufficient alternative to sandwiches)
- teapots with cosies accompanied by a pot of hot water to replenish the pot (an English tradition)
- often served on two- or three-tiered china cake plates or pedestal plates

We have occasionally been asked about the difference between afternoon tea and high tea. High tea is often mistakenly thought of as an elaborate, elegant version of afternoon tea. In fact, in England, it is a different, much less elegant, meal served a little later for those who are unable to take a late afternoon break. It is a merging of afternoon tea and a main meal. In northern England, sandwiches are replaced with a knife and fork course often consisting of cold sliced ham, scotch eggs, veal, ham and pork pie, and salad; however, grilled gammon or something similar may also be served. Sliced buttered bread, cakes, scones, squares, biscuits and even trifle complete the meal.

At the end of this book, we have listed books about Afternoon Tea which we have found to be most helpful.

# Table of Contents

# TABLE OF CONTENTS

# *The Prairie Elevator*

**Main Street
Acadia Valley, AB   T0J 0A0
(403) 972-2028**

*Managed by the Prairie Elevator Society*

Located on Highway #41 north of Medicine Hat. Watch for signs when you enter Acadia Valley on Main Street.

The Prairie Elevator is wheelchair accessible, with stairs to the tea house. Refreshments will be brought to a picnic table or to a wheelchair if requested. Ample parking is available.

*Hours:*     Open from the May to October long weekends, July and August from 10:00 a.m. to 5:00 p.m. Weekends only from mid-May to the end of June, and from September to mid-October

*MENU:*

Includes a wide selection of specialty teas, coffee and juices such as Saskatoon berry and wild blackberry (chokecherry). Home-baked items vary daily and include tarts, muffins, cakes, and squares.

*DECOR:*

The tea room building was originally the elevator office. Country-style decor is accentuated with giftware and crafts displayed on the walls and shelves, brightly coloured table cloths, wooden chairs, and lace curtains.

Gift items unique to the prairies are available for sale as well as a large selection of arts and crafts.

*HISTORY:*

The original elevator was destroyed in a fire and rebuilt in 1968. It ceased to be a working elevator in 1989 and was then purchased from Alberta Wheat Pool by the Municipal District of Acadia and saved from demolition. A group of volunteers decided to open it to the public as a tourist attraction.

The elevator houses various museum pieces relating to the grain-growing industry. Visitors are invited to either a guided tour or a self-guided tour with a video presentation on the workings of an elevator as to how grain was delivered, stored, and shipped from the prairie.

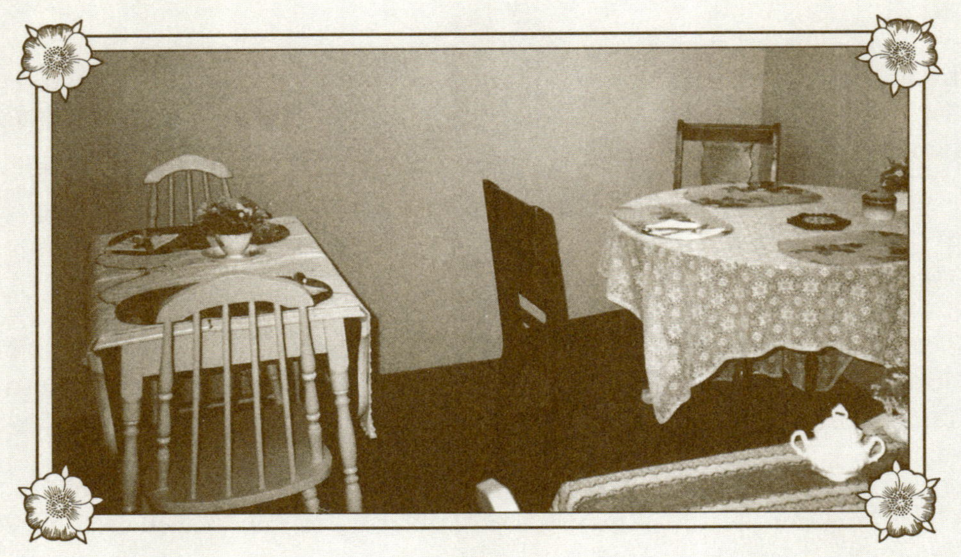

# NOSTALGIA SHOPPE AND TEA HOUSE

**4728 – 50A Street
Alberta Beach, AB   T0E 0A0
(403) 924-3654**

*Judy Muir, Owner*

Alberta Beach is located on Lac Ste. Anne. From Highway #16 West, take Highway #43 north; 10 km north, turn left onto Highway #633. The Nostalgia Shoppe is in a small house in the residential section of Alberta Beach, two blocks east of the hotel, facing a baseball diamond.

The tea house is not wheelchair accessible. Parking is available on the street.

*Hours:*     Tuesday to Sunday from 11:00 a.m. to 5:00 p.m. between April and October, including holiday Mondays at the above times (depending on how soon winter arrives)

*MENU:*

Light meal and snack choices include soup, muffins, and daily desserts. Scones and biscuits are baked on an old coal and wood stove. Various flavours of teas and coffees are also available.

*DECOR:*

The dining room is furnished with a variety of collectible and antique tables and chairs. Dressers and display cabinets brim over with a large assortment of china items, lamps, glassware, homemade crafts, and other collectibles. Pictures and plates decorate the walls. All of these items are for sale, with the exception of those in the dining room.

*HISTORY:*

The building was originally a summer lake cottage built sometime during the 1940s or 1950s. It was later extended and redecorated with old wallpapers.

# THE TEA HOUSE

**Wye Road and Range Road #221**
**Ardrossan, AB   T8E 2G7**
**(403) 922-6963**

*Marlene Lothian, Manager/Owner*

Located at Wye Road in Sherwood Park and Range Road #221.

The tea room is not wheelchair accessible. Ample parking is available at the front of the house.

*HOURS:*        Monday to Friday from 11:00 a.m. to 4:00 p.m.
Saturday and Sunday from 11:00 a.m. to 5:00 p.m.

*MENU:*

The Tea House's specialty is Welsh tea cakes served with thick cream and jam, for $3.50.

The menu also offers two types of sandwiches and two kinds of soup daily, as well as a hot entrée. Soup or sandwich items may be ordered with a salad, or a combination of all three (soup, salad, and sandwich). Desserts are served anytime.

Various teas, herbal and regular, are offered as well as coffee, juice, milk, floats, sodas, and blueberry tea.

*DECOR:*

Flower-filled tea pots highlight the steps up to the front veranda. The inside of the tea house is decorated with various antiques and collectibles. There is seating for approximately 30 people and reservations are recommended. Additional entertainment includes a Murder Mystery Dinner theatre, tea leaf reading (by appointment), reflexology and watercolour lessons.

*HISTORY:*

Built in 1906, the tea house was the Canadian Imperial Bank of Commerce building in Vegreville and was moved to its present site in 1992, avoiding the bulldozer. The original fixtures, such as the solid oak mantel, the front entry door, kitchen cupboards, dining room chandelier, and the bathtub, have been restored to provide many more years of use. An expansion to the upper floor and to the exterior of the building is planned for the future.

The Treasure Chest Antiques shop located across the parking lot offers a wide selection of handmade crafts, antiques, and collectibles. This old building was once the Garden School House, serving the community for many years.

# WHEATHEART CROFT TEA ROOM

**Main Street**
**Barons, AB   T0L 0G0**
**(403) 757-3820 or 757-2112**

***Contacts: Dee Ryrie, Carol Noble, Judie Allen***

Located on Highway #23, 39 kilometres northwest of Lethbridge.

The tea room is not wheelchair accessible (there is one small step into the tea house). Ample parking is available on the street.

*HOURS:*       Summer – May to September
Tuesday to Sunday from 12:00 noon to 5:00 p.m.

Off Season – October to April
Saturday and Sunday from 1:00 p.m. to 5:00 p.m.

Christmas Season – December 15 to 24
12:00 noon to 5:00 p.m. daily

*MENU:*

The Wheatheart Croft offers its visitors a variety of teas and treats.


*DECOR:*

French doors, a fireplace, original fixtures, and tables set for tea are enhanced by gifts on display.

A gift shop on site features handcrafted, locally-made arts and crafts such as paintings, quilts, pottery, dried flower arrangements, and other crafts.


*HISTORY:*

This delightful tea house and gift shop is located on Main Street in Barons, off Highway #23. Originally serving as the Barons Post Office and postmaster's residence, this structure was designated an historic site in 1995. It was built by Postmaster Alex Andrew in 1923, in a style reminiscent of his Scottish homeland. The red brick exterior with white trim reflects the warmth and charm of a Scottish cottage and also reflects Mr. Andrew's trade as a bricklayer prior to the first World War in Scotland.

# Verna's Tea House

**Main Street**
**Bittern Lake, AB   T0C 0L0**
**(403) 672-0818**

*Verna Lindholm, Owner*

Located on Highway #13, approximately 25 km east of Wetaskiwin and 15 km west of Camrose.

The tea room is wheelchair accessible. There is ample street parking.

*Hours:*        Monday to Saturday from 6:30 a.m. to 9:45 p.m.
               Closed Sunday

All menu items are homemade. Daily soup and sandwich lunch specials are served all day starting at 11:00 a.m. A different soup is featured each day, such as split pea, turkey, corn chowder, beef and barley, clam chowder, and hamburger.

All sandwiches are made to order on either a homemade open-faced bun or sliced homemade bread. A variety of sandwich fillings are available such as chicken, ham, and beef, all home cooked and sliced straight from the roast. Other fillings include turkey, tuna salad, and tuna melt.

Suppers are served family style and feature a different special each day; soup or salad and a hot vegetable are included. Hot, open-faced sandwiches and family-style meals are served during the supper hour between 5:00 p.m. and 7:00 p.m.

Desserts include pie, with or without Schwan's ice cream, seasonal fruit pies such as sour cream raisin, Dutch apple, lemon meringue, and rhubarb sponge. Chocolate or strawberry ice cream pies, blueberry or carrot-pineapple jumbo muffins, butter tarts, and servings of Schwan's ice cream are also available.

Beverages include coffee, regular and specialty teas, milk, iced tea and real fruit punch.

## *DECOR:*

The atmosphere is casual and friendly. Tables with umbrellas are set up on the front lawn during warmer weather. Original paintings by local artists are displayed and are for sale.

## *HISTORY:*

Built in 1927, this building has served as a town office and a post office. Walking trails along Bittern Lake are accessible nearby.

# NESTLE INN BED AND BREAKFAST AND TEA ROOM

P.O. Box 1225
12313 – 21 Avenue
Crowsnest Pass
Blairmore, AB   T0K 0E0
(403) 562-2474

*P. Dana-Vogt, Proprietor*

Located on 21 Avenue between 123 and 125 Street.

The tea house is not wheelchair accessible. Parking is available on the street.

*HOURS:*  Open year-round, Monday to Friday
from 11:00 a.m. to 4:00 p.m.
Tea room closed Saturday and Sunday
Bed and Breakfast open 7 days a week

## *MENU:*

Menu items feature daily specials, homemade soups, deli sandwiches, pastries, desserts, and gourmet salads. Beverages include coffee, cappuccino, espresso, pop, and over 15 varieties of specialty teas.

## *DECOR:*

The tea room seats 25 people inside and eight people on an outside deck; a private dining room seating up to eight people is also available. A fireplace adds to the coziness and warm atmosphere in the tea room. The country-Victorian decor is accentuated by antiques and collectibles.

## *HISTORY:*

This cozy and unique structure was one of the original homes built in the area in 1915. It was built for the "Mine Bosses." A brick and oak hearth and the original heavy oak beams on the ceiling add warmth and character to the main floor fireside guest parlour.

# Conversations Tea Room and Restaurant

**10816 MacLeod Trail South**
**224 Willowpark Village**
**Calgary, AB   T2J 5N8**
**(403) 271-8886**

*Marlene Duxbury, Owner*

Located in the city of Calgary on MacLeod Trail South.

The tea room is wheelchair accessible. Parking is available on the front street.

**HOURS:**     Monday to Saturday from 9:00 a.m. to 11:00 p.m.
Sunday from 10:00 a.m. to 3:00 p.m.

*MENU:*

Homemade soups, baked goods, fresh salads, and creative lunch and dinner entrées ensure that there will be something for everyone. "Heart smart" menu items are available on the lunch menu. Daily special afternoon treats include muffins and a decadent dessert of the day. Dinner choices feature continental dishes of beef, chicken, and pasta. Several specialty egg dishes and a choice of specialty salads and crêpes are served for Sunday brunch. A breakfast special includes fresh tomato and avocado slices topped with poached eggs and Hollandaise sauce; fresh fruit and a scone complete the plate.

All items on the menu are available for take-out service. Trays filled with sandwiches, hors d'oeuvres, desserts, and fruits and cheeses can be ordered ahead. If you bring in one of your own fancy bowls, they will fill it with a fresh salad.

*DECOR:*

The dining room is full of country charm. Flowered wallpaper and pale wooden tables and chairs accentuate the slate blue and dusty rose colours used throughout the tea room.

# CAMROSE RAILWAY STATION AND TEA ROOM

**44th Street and 47th Avenue**
**P.O. Box 1174**
**Camrose, AB   T4V 1X2**
**(403) 672-3099**

*Operated by the Canadian Northern Society*

Located 45 minutes southeast of Edmonton.

This tea room is seasonally wheelchair accessible. Please phone ahead for more information. Ample parking is available.

*HOURS:*     Open from April 15 to November 30
Monday to Saturday from 10:00 a.m. to 5:00 p.m.

For June, July, and August only
Additional hours include
Sunday from 1:00 p.m. to 4:00 p.m.

*MENU*

The tea room serves light lunches, homemade desserts, and coffee for 25¢ a cup! Hot beverages include flavoured coffees, specialty and flavoured teas, hot apple cider, and hot chocolate. Cold beverages include milk, iced tea, pink lemonade, juices, floats, and milk shakes. Homemade desserts such as muffins, pie, carrot cake, brownies, pumpkin loaf, banana bread, cinnamon buns, chocolate cheesecake, ice cream, sherbet, and "Steam Train" flavored gelatins are also available.

Light lunches of sandwiches, salads, and a hot daily special such as chili or stew are featured, and all-day snacks of toast, nachos, and corn dogs are available. Soup and other hot daily specials are also offered.

After hours bookings and private reservations are available upon request for birthdays, meetings, reunions, and small parties.

*DECOR:*

The tea room has a unique atmosphere and displays authentic Canadian Railway memorabilia. Natural wood tables add to the old-style charm of the tea room.

*HISTORY:*

This historic railway station was built in 1911 as a Canadian Northern Standard 3rd Class Depot. In the 1950s, the station underwent expansion and development and now stands as an expanded 3rd class depot. The station operated under Canadian National until its closure in 1988. It is now owned and operated by the Canadian Northern Society, a nonprofit, registered, charitable organization dedicated to the preservation and promotion of Canadian National Railways' heritage and historic structures in western Canada. The tea room is in the original railway station. Camrose was once home to three railway lines that included the Canadian National, Canadian Pacific, and the Grand Trunk Pacific. A gift shop, railway library, and museum are also in the building, along with a telegraph office where old photographs, timetables, posters, and other artifacts are on display.

# THE RUFFINGTON TEA ROOM

**4803 – 48 Street
Camrose, AB   T4V IL4
(403) 672-4500**

*D'Arcy Arial, Coral Eklund, Karen Ofrim, Owners
Coral Eklund, Manager*

Located 45 minutes southeast of Edmonton.

The tea room is not wheelchair accessible. Parking is available in front of the store and also at the back.

*Hours:* Open Monday to Saturday from 10:00 a.m. to 5:30 p.m.
Sunday during the summer from 1:00 p.m. to 4:00 p.m.

*MENU:*

Lunch items include sandwiches on homemade bread. A good assortment of muffins, pastries, cheesecakes, and a variety of home-baked scones are available. Beverages include lemonade, iced tea, regular and decaffeinated coffee and tea, various herbal teas, specialty coffees, and several flavours of hot chocolate.

*DECOR:*

The tea room is furnished with a mix and match of antique pine furniture, original paintings, dried flowers, cookery books, jams, hand-painted glass vases, painted wooden serviette holders, welcome signs, and pictures, all adding a touch of nostalgia. Consignment items from the gift shop, such as dried flowers, pottery, wood and fabric crafts, pictures and more, help to create a cozy atmosphere. Patio doors and large floor-to-ceiling windows draped with Battenburg lace open onto a lovely private patio for outdoor summer seating.

*HISTORY:*

This two-storey, vintage home is situated in an historic district of Camrose and also contains a gift store with hand-crafted gifts and a fudge factory.

# THE *N.W.M.P.* BARRACKS TEA ROOM AND *MUSEUM*

**Main Street
Canmore, AB   T0L 0M0
(403) 678-1955**

*Operated by the Centennial Museum Society of Canmore*

Canmore is 45 minutes west of Calgary off Highway #1 and a few minutes' drive east of Banff National Park gates.

The tea room is wheelchair accessible. Parking is available on the street.

*Hours:*   July and August open daily from 12:00 noon to 4:00 p.m. The rest of the year on Saturday and Sunday from 1:00 p.m. to 4:00 p.m.

Homemade cake and cookies, tea, and other refreshments are featured.

*DECOR:*

The museum is furnished in a 1920s style, and the atmosphere is casual and friendly.

*HISTORY:*

In 1892, a plot of land on the west bank of Policeman's Creek was chosen as the site for the North West Mounted Police building. Two policemen and their horses lived there after construction of the barracks and a stable was completed in 1893. When the detachment moved across the river, in 1928, the building sat empty until 1930, when it was first rented then sold to a local man. The stable was demolished in 1943, but the old, mud-chinked, log structure was left intact. This building still stands by the creek at the east end of Main Street.

Many pictures and other N.W.M.P. memorabilia are on display in the Barracks. Members of the Centennial Museum Society are on hand and willingly answer any questions visitors may have. Special tours of the museum are also available. Phone (403) 678-2462 for more information.

The Society has completely restored the building, which was recently acquired by the Town of Canmore. Restoration was completed by the Society with the assistance of the Alberta Historical Resources Foundation.

# *PaSu Farm Bed and Breakfast*

**P.O. Box 656
Carstairs, AB   T0M 0N0
(403) 337-2800**

***Pat and Sue de Rosemond, Owners***

Located on Highway #580 off of Highway #2A, 45 minutes northwest of Calgary, southwest of Carstairs.

The farm is wheelchair accessible. Ample parking is available.

*Hours:*   Tuesday to Wednesday from 10:00 a.m. to 5:00 p.m.

Thursday, Friday & Saturday from 10:00 a.m. to 10:00 p.m. (Fine dining offered these days. Reservations essential as special events may cancel supper service.)

Friday and Saturday evenings – Special Events nights

Sunday from 12:00 noon to 5:00 p.m.
Closed Monday

Lunch is served from 11:30 a.m. to 3:00 p.m.
Tuesday to Friday
Buffet Carvery is served from 12:00 noon to 2:30 p.m.
every Sunday

Soups, salads, sandwiches, quiche, Ploughman's lunch, shepherd's pie, venison, roast beef, lamb chops, and omelettes are served for lunch. Desserts include scones with clotted, fresh cream and preserves, cheese cake, fresh baked pies, devil's torte, English trifle, and fresh fruit salad. Coffee, cappuccino, espresso, caffè latte, regular, herbal, and fruit teas, pop, and orange juice are available. The restaurant specializes in fine foods with fresh ingredients such as extra virgin cold pressed olive oil, balsamic, and other fine vinegars. Fresh bread is baked every day and served with all meals. On Sundays, a superb carvery featuring roast beef and lamb is offered. Friday and Saturday nights are devoted to Dinner Theatres or other special entertainment. Special themes are featured throughout the year, such as Valentine's evening, gourmet supper club, and a Medieval evening. Bookings for banquets, weddings, private functions, and personalized menus are available. Meals are moderately priced and dress is casual to formal.

## *DECOR:*

The chateau-style cottage looks out over the green rolling hills to the Rocky Mountains. A gallery features fine sheepskin and wool products such as slippers, mittens, dress gloves, vests, hats, and sweaters. Other items for sale are tapestries from Swaziland, African carvings, candles, beads, and jewellery. A mail-order service is available.

## *HISTORY:*

Pat and Sue de Rosemond first purchased the land in 1979 with the goal of running a small sheep farm. In 1980, the barn was burned down to make way for the Quonset, which was divided into a home and a lambing barn for the sheep. The sale of their wool became a very successful venture; by 1986, they were doing shows and fairs from Montreal to Vancouver. In 1987, the barn portion of the Quonset was turned into the present shop and served as a restaurant and tea room. In 1992, the present restaurant was built and was turned into a full restaurant in 1994. PaSu Farm is a working sheep farm. Scheduled tours are welcome for those who wish to learn how wool is sheared, washed, dyed, carded, and spun. Children and adults can touch, pet, and feed the lambs and sheep.

# TEA AND TREASURES

**5117 Victoria Avenue
Coronation, AB   T0C 1C0
(403) 578-2299**

*Amber Swahn, Colleen Brown, Rowena Swahn, Managers*

Located on Highway #12, southeast of Stettler.

The tea house is wheelchair accessible. Parking is available at the front and rear of the house.

*HOURS:*   Monday to Saturday from 11:00 a.m. to 5:00 p.m.
Sunday and statutory holidays from
12:00 p.m. to 4:00 p.m.

Lunch, served daily between 11:00 a.m. and 2:00 p.m., includes homemade desserts such as pies, squares, cakes, doughnuts, and cookies. Children's portions are available.

Beverages include regular, flavoured, and herbal teas, regular and flavoured coffees, as well as iced tea, lemonade, hot chocolate, mocha, milk, and pop.

Made-to-order cakes and other homemade items may be purchased.

Reservations are taken for various private and social functions, and educational classes. Various theme parties are also available throughout the year such as Christmas, Easter, and Valentine's Day.

*DECOR:*

The two-storey house is decorated in Victorian style. Its character is accentuated by hardwood floors, stained-glass windows, and a large veranda. A variety of items made by local craftspeople are for sale on both the main and upper floors and include homemade preserves, wooden furnishings, clothing, bedding, and porcelain dolls. A room containing dolls from 1925 to the present completes the varied list of items available for viewing. Collectibles, crafts, and a year-round Christmas room are on the second floor.

*HISTORY:*

The house was built in 1926 in Consort, Alberta, by a bachelor for his wife-to-be. When the wedding did not take place, he lived there on his own. The house was moved to Coronation by the present owners.

# Tea Tyme and Porcelain Pleasures

**4901 King Street**
**Coronation, AB   T0C 1C0**
**(403) 578-2376**

*Edna Redelback, Manager*

Located in Coronation, on Highway #12, approximately 94 km east of Stettler.

The tea room is wheelchair accessible. Parking is available in lots on either side of the building.

*HOURS:*        Daily from 10:00 a.m. to 5:00 p.m.

The lunch menu features salads, soup, sandwiches, stews, chili, Cornish pasties, lasagna, homemade desserts, and a variety of teas.

## *DECOR:*

The tea room is decorated in a pretty pink and floral theme against a white background with white lace tablecloths covering the tables. A refinished cupboard dating back to the early 1900s is on display replete with antique cups, saucers, and unusual teapots. A large built-in cabinet displays some of the porcelain dolls made by the owner; a partner makes the doll clothes and teddy bears, which are for sale.

Giftware and jewellery items made by local artists are for sale, as well as souvenirs and a mug with a specially designed decal. Tea Tyme caters to small social gatherings. Those celebrating birthdays receive a tea-bag holder made by the manager. Classes are offered for those wishing to make their own dolls.

## *HISTORY:*

The tea room opened on November 3, 1995. The building was designed by the manager and built by her son.

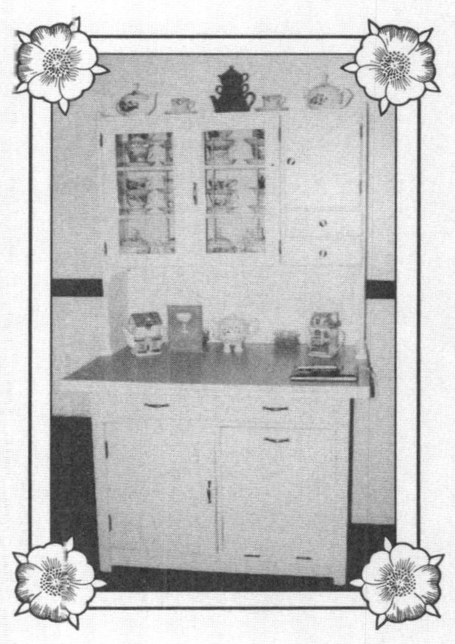

# Cornwall Cottage Tea Garden

**Box 1110**
**30 Huron Street**
**Devon, AB   T0C 1E0**
**(403) 987-2121**

*Linda Stewart, Rhonda Stewart, Owners/Managers*

Located southwest of Edmonton. Take Highway #16X west to Highway #60 (Devon turnoff). Turn south. The teahouse is located near the Esso station and can be seen from the highway.

The tea house is wheelchair accessible. Ample parking is available.

*Hours:* *Winter*   Sunday to Thursday from
11:00 a.m. to 8:00 p.m.

Friday and Saturday from
11:00 a.m. to 9:00 p.m.

*Summer*   11:00 a.m. to 10:00 p.m. daily

Tea and scones are served all day.

Afternoon Tea consists of:

| | |
|---|---|
| Scones | $2.25 |
| Fruit pie | $3.75 |
| à la mode | $1.00 |

Tea, coffee, herbal and iced teas, hot chocolate, hot apple cider, juice, and milk are also offered. Tea is served in tea pots with tea cosies, hand-knitted by the mother-in-law of one of the proprietors.

The Tea Garden also serves a midmorning treat of huge cinnamon buns and muffins. Soups, salads, sandwiches, and desserts are available for lunch, with the addition of roast beef with Yorkshire pudding and shepherd's pie with salad for dinner.

*DECOR:*

The atmosphere is friendly, pleasant, and informal with dried flower arrangements, bric-à-brac, and an old gas stove in a fireplace alcove. A patio area is located outside for warm, sunny days. Pretty flowers border the building on the south and west sides during the summer months.

Cornwall Cottage Crafts is a newly opened craft store located next to the tea garden. Wares are from local crafters including a woodworker who specializes in making bird houses. Other items for sale include antique furniture, silk paintings, pottery, and paper tole. The shop is open daily from 11:00 a.m. to 4:00 p.m.

*HISTORY:*

The Tea Garden building was originally constructed as a government conservation office after the Leduc #1 oil strike in 1947. The original site of the strike is a few minutes' drive south of Devon on Highway #60. The building has also served as a private residence and as the office of several businesses, including the field office for the Energy Resources Conservation Board between 1948 and 1966.

# CAFE EUROPA

**Europa Boulevard**
**West Edmonton Mall**
**17700 – 87 Avenue**
**Edmonton, AB   T5T 4V4**
**(403) 444-5396    Toll Free: 1-800-661-6454**

*Gloria Gallant, Manager*

Located in the city of Edmonton at West Edmonton Mall. Take 170 Street to 90 Avenue, turn west. Park near Entrance #1, Upper Level, 172 Street and 90 Avenue (Europa Boulevard entrance).

The cafe is wheelchair accessible. There is ample parking in the parkade.

*Hours:*   The restaurant is open from 7:00 a.m. to 9:00 p.m.

Afternoon tea is served daily between
2:30 p.m. and 5:00 p.m.

*MENU:*

Afternoon tea is served on a three-tiered plate accompanied by a Sadler's brown-betty tea pot and includes:
freshly baked scones
assorted pastries
chocolate-dipped fruit
$5.95 per person

Tea selections include orange pekoe, Earl Grey, various fruit, herbal, and decaffeinated varieties (Mint Melody, Orange and Spice, and Apple Orchard).

Luncheon and supper menu items are also available ranging from sandwiches, soup, salads, several English-style entrées, and daily specials.

*DECOR:*

This cafe offers a European-style decor and is located in the old-world area of the mall called Europa Boulevard.

# THE HOTEL MACDONALD

**The Harvest Room**
**10065 – 100 Street**
**Edmonton, AB   T5J 0N6**
**(403) 424-5181**

Located in downtown Edmonton.

Parking is available at the hotel and at nearby parkades. The hotel is wheelchair accessible.

*HOURS:*   Monday to Friday from 6:30 a.m. to 10:00 p.m.
Saturday and Sunday from 7:00 a.m. to 5:30 p.m.
Closed daily from 2:00 p.m. to 5:30 p.m.

Afternoon Tea is served from 3:00 p.m. to 5:00 p.m.
between the May to September long weekends, at
Christmas time, and on Family Day in February.

*MENU:*

Afternoon tea is served on a 3-tiered china cake plate and consists of:
> 2 scones with strawberry compote and Jersey cream
> Finger sandwiches with a variety of fillings
> English afternoon pastries
> A pot of brewed tea each, your choice of flavour
> $12.95 per person
>
> Two scones with strawberry compote and Jersey cream
> A pot of brewed tea each, your choice of flavour
> $6.50 per person

The restaurant also offers breakfast, lunch, and dinner menus. Beverages include specialty teas such as China Black, Blackberry, and Mint Soother, as well as espresso, cappuccino, caffè latte, and café mocha.


*DECOR:*

The Harvest Room features outstanding views of the North Saskatchewan River Valley and a unique open-kitchen design which enhances its West Coast theme. There are seasonal decorations at appropriate times of the year. Seasonally, afternoon tea is also served on the patio overlooking the hotel gardens and the North Saskatchewan River.


*HISTORY:*

The Hotel Macdonald was named a Municipal Historic Resource by the City of Edmonton in 1985. One of Edmonton's finest hotels, the "Mac" was also Edmonton's centre of social activity. Designed with an exterior structure similar to that of a sixteenth-century French castle, the interior is reminiscent of the castle of a Scottish laird. The turrets and other European features have come to symbolize the Canadian railway hotels and characterize many of today's Canadian Pacific Hotels and Resorts across Canada.

Closed in 1983, the hotel was bought by Canadian Pacific Hotels in 1988. It has been recently restored at a cost of $28 million. Reopened in 1991, it has been returned to its former elegance, reestablishing its tradition of excellence in service and hospitality in the Edmonton area.

# NELLIE'S TEA SHOPPE

**12606 – 118 Avenue**
**Edmonton, AB   T5L 2K0**
**(403) 452-9429**

*Tom and Nellie White, Owners*

The Tea Shoppe is located five blocks west of Edmonton Municipal Airport on 118 Avenue.

The Tea Shoppe is wheelchair accessible. There is parking at the rear of the building.

**HOURS:**     Monday to Thursday from 11:00 a.m. to 10:00 p.m.
Friday and Saturday from 11:00 a.m. to 11:00 p.m.
Sunday from 10:00 a.m. to 10:00 p.m.
Afternoon tea is served between 2:30 p.m. and 5:00 p.m.

Reservations are required for afternoon tea, which costs $10.95 per person, and includes a selection of open-faced sandwiches, scones with clotted cream, preserves, tea loaf, fresh fruit, and a pot of tea. The tea is served in a three-tiered plate with sterling silver cutlery.

A smaller tea, at a cost of $6.95 per person, is comprised of scones, clotted cream, preserves, and choice of tea.

Other menu choices feature soups, sandwiches, quiche, salads, full-course meals, cheesecakes, tortes, and pies, and a selection of various hot and cold beverages. A Sunday brunch, lunch, and dinner specials are also available.

*DECOR:*

Decorated in a blue and white motif and accentuated by Dutch pottery items, the tea shoppe is reminiscent of grandma's living room. Wood panelling, a fireplace, folding screens, brassware, clocks, pictures, lamps, potted plants, and other collectible items create a cosy, welcoming atmosphere.

# *The Friends of Rutherford House Tea Room*

**Rutherford House Provincial Historic Site**
**11153 Saskatchewan Drive**
**Edmonton, AB   T6G 2S1**
**(403) 422-2697**

***Operated by the Friends of Rutherford Society***

Located on the south side of the Saskatchewan River in Edmonton.

The building is wheelchair accessible. Parking is available on Saskatchewan Drive.

*Hours:*       Wednesday to Sunday 11:30 a.m. to 4:00 p.m.

*MENU:*          A variety of selections include:

*Lunch:*          Hot savouries, soups, sandwiches, salads, plough-
                 man's lunch, pastries, and dessert specials.

*Afternoon Tea:*  English-cut scones, sweet tea breads,
                 fresh baking, and fruit.

*Beverages:*      Large selection of herbal and regular teas; coffee,
                 cider, and lemonade.

## DECOR:

Lunch and afternoon tea are served in the breakfast nook, den, and sun porch of Rutherford House. Cosy furniture and a view of the west lawns make the sun porch a particularly inviting stop. Each table is set with linens, fine china, and silverware. Reservations are recommended for the tea room and are necessary for afternoon tea.

The house has been refurbished to its original 1915 grandeur. Declared an historic site in 1973, the house is now open to the public for guided interpretive tours. Edwardian dress is worn by the hostesses and interpreters in the house. Staff and volunteers help to recreate household activities. Reenactments of important events in the Rutherfords' lives are also presented.

## HISTORY:

Rutherford House was the home of Dr. Alexander Cameron Rutherford and his family, wife Mattie, daughter Hazel, and son Cecil, from 1911 to 1940. Located on the University of Alberta Campus, the house overlooks the North Saskatchewan River. Dr. Rutherford is an important figure in Edmonton's and Alberta's history as the first Premier of Alberta and the founder of the University of Alberta. The Rutherfords named their home "Achnacarry" after the ancestral home of the clan Cameron.

This Edwardian house was once the centre of many social activities, hosting the elite of Edmonton. Politicians and other well-known community members were often the guests at lavish dinner parties held by Mrs. Rutherford. The Rutherfords were the first to employ maids and servants in Edmonton.

# *Treasures and Tea*
# *Victorian Gift Shop*
# *and Restaurant*

**520 Riverbend Square**
**Terwilligar Drive and Rabbit Hill Road**
**Edmonton, AB   T6R 2E3**
**(403) 438-1737**

*Claudia Zeigler, Proprietor*

Located in southwest Edmonton. Take Whitemud Drive to Terwilligar Drive. Turn west onto Terwilligar and follow it to Rabbit Hill Road. Turn north. Tea room located in a small mall.

The tea room is wheelchair accessible. Ample parking is available at the front of the building.

*Hours:*  Monday to Saturday from 10:00 a.m. to 5:00 p.m.
Sunday from 11:00 a.m. to 2:00 p.m.
Afternoon Tea served daily from 2:30 p.m.

Afternoon Tea à la carte:
        Scones, cream, and jam. . . . . . . . . . . $2.75
        Finger sandwiches . . . . . . . . . . . . . . $4.95
        (different fillings daily)
        Pastry plates. . . . . . . . . . . . . . . . . . $4.95

Afternoon Tea:
        assorted sandwiches and pastries
        your choice of tea
        $7.50 each or
        $14.50 for two

Mad Hatter Tea Party (children only):
        a happy-face sandwich
        sweet treats
        choice of beverage
        $3.95 per person

The restaurant also serves breakfast, lunch, dinner, and Sunday brunch.


*DECOR:*

The Victoriana theme is enhanced by Battenberg lace window hangings and handmade floral arrangements. The tables are decorated with dried flowers, flower-pattern table mats, and linens.

An attached gift shop offers a varied selection of Victoriana including pretty notelets, dried flower arrangements, scented candles, table linens, and assorted books. Other items for sale include candlesticks, table mats, tea cosies, aprons, Battenberg lace items, books, toys, and other novelties.

# DUNVEGAN GARDENS AND TEA ROOM

**Box 514**
**Fairview, AB   T0H 1L0**
**(403) 835-4459**

*Ron and Pauline Friesen, Owners*

Located 90 km north of Grande Prairie on Highway #2, east of Dunvegan Park and Dunvegan Bridge.

The tea room is wheelchair accessible. Grandma's Attic gift area is not. Ample parking is available outside the greenhouse.

*HOURS:*     Open after Easter until Christmas
Monday to Saturday from 10:00 a.m. to 9:00 p.m.
Sunday from 1:00 p.m. to 9:00 p.m.
Reservations are recommended

Morning coffee is served with homemade bread or scones with jam, muffins, and cinnamon buns. Lunch includes homemade soups, salads, burgers, Teriyaki or barbecue chicken sandwiches, and a daily sandwich special. Daily dinner specials feature steak sandwich, "Chish and Phipps," ethnic specialties such as Tandoori chicken and moussaka, and various seafood and chicken dishes. Desserts include homemade pies, specialty cakes, dessert crêpes, cheesecakes, and several ice cream specialties. Dunvegan desserts are noncalorific if you run up the hill afterwards. (So claims their menu!)

Tea is served in English china tea pots; varieties include specialty fruit, herb teas, as well as Earl Grey and green teas. Coffee, juices, ice tea, milk shakes, and floats are also available.

## *DECOR:*

The tea room is located in the barn adjoining the greenhouse, giving it a rustic, country atmosphere. During the summer months, picnic tables with umbrellas are set up outside. The tea room can be booked for weddings, reunions, parties, meetings, and birthdays. Grandma's Attic is located above the tea room and features a mix of country, Victorian, and antique gifts and furniture. Bulk teas, souvenirs, homemade preserves, and Dunvegan Hill honey are available. Gift certificates can be purchased upon request.

## *HISTORY:*

The name comes from Dunvegan castle, the ancestral home of the clan MacLeod on the Isle of Skye, off the west coast of Scotland. Dunvegan Gardens, started in 1952 by Bill and Hilda Friesen, grows scrumptious vegetables and strawberries, as well as a wide variety of bedding plants.

# THE OLD BARN STORE AND TEA HOUSE

**Box 1185**
**Grande Prairie, AB   T8V 4B6**
**(403) 532-3212**

*David and Betty Friesen, Owners/Managers*

Located at the Dunvegan Gardens, 3 km south of Grande Prairie on Highway #40.

The tea room and gift shop are not wheelchair accessible. Parking is available on site.

*Hours:*     Monday to Saturday from 10:00 a.m. to 5:00 p.m.
Closed Sunday

*MENU:*

Light lunch menu items include soup with your choice of Johnny cake, croissant, or a sandwich. Main-course selections feature lasagna, fish and chips, pot pies, chicken fingers with fries, burgers, and chicken sandwiches. Desserts include freshly baked pies, cheesecakes, and German chocolate cake.

A selection of teas, including flavoured and caffeine-free fruit varieties, as well as coffee, milk, chocolate milk, juices, and soft drinks, is available.

*DECOR:*

Rich burgundy and hunter-green decor complements the natural pine floor giving the tea house a Victorian-country atmosphere. Plenty of windows allow an abundance of natural light into the tea room, making it bright and pleasant.

Accessible by a spiral staircase, the tea room has seating capacity for up to 40 people and includes an outdoor balcony and a unique top-of-the-silo alcove. A gift shop is also located at the top of the staircase and offers an extensive selection of items for sale including giftware, antiques, linens, fine china, and much more.

*HISTORY:*

Dunvegan Gardens is one of two nursery gardens and tea room establishments owned by the Friesens in the Peace Country. The Grande Prairie tea room opened March 2, 1995.

# THE DOLL PALACE TEA ROOM AND GIFT SHOP

**400 Pioneer Trail
Hanna, AB   T1J 1P0
(403) 854-2756**

*Violetta Link, Owner*

Located on the east side of Hanna, off Highway #9, 82 km northeast of Drumheller.

The house is wheelchair accessible. Ample parking is available.

*HOURS:*        Open daily from 9:00 a.m. to 9:00 p.m.

## *MENU:*

All items on the menu are homemade and include soup and sandwiches, cinnamon buns, pies, tarts, tea, and coffee. A buffet is offered
every Sunday and a hot special is served daily during the winter.

## *DECOR:*

The tea room can seat 48 people. A collection of over 2500 dolls is on
display. Admission for the display is $4.00 for adults, $1.00 for children
7 and under (must be accompanied by an adult). The dolls are made
by over 70 doll companies and date from the early 1900s to present
day. Bus tours and special bookings are available.

Handmade crafts and other consignment items from the local community are found throughout the tea room.

## *HISTORY:*

The proprietors had farmed for
37 years when they decided to
try something different. In May
1993, property was purchased in
Hanna, and a new building was
built to display the dolls and
house a tea room.

# FOREVER COUNTRY ANTIQUES AND COLLECTIBLES

**Box 379**
**Hardisty, AB   T0B 1V0**
**(403) 888-2291**

*Lori Goodrich and Bonnie Whidden, Owners*

Located in Hardisty just off Highway #13, 112 km southeast of Camrose. Forever Country is located on Highway #881, south of Hardisty.

The house is wheelchair accessible. Parking is available on the street.

*Hours:*     April 1 to August 31 open Monday to Friday from 9:00 a.m. to 5:30 p.m.
Saturday from 10:00 a.m. to 5:30 p.m.

September 1 to March 31, open weekdays from 9:00 a.m. to 4:30 p.m.
Saturday from 10:00 a.m. to 4:30 p.m.

*MENU:*

Menu items featured are tea, coffee, and a daily sweet.


*DECOR:*

The tea room reflects the early 1900s atmosphere of the entire house, which includes a dining room, parlour, bedrooms, nursery, and bath. There is a "gingerbread" veranda adjoining the house.

On the first weekend of November each year, the owners host Christmas Tree Days, displaying many lovely Christmas decorations and gifts. The house is closed on the previous Friday to prepare the rooms and decorate with Christmas items. Please phone for information regarding hours for this event.


*HISTORY:*

The two-storey house dates from 1914 and was built by Allan Johnstone, who owned the lumber yard in Hardisty. A feature wall displays historical facts and memorabilia from the beginnings of Hardisty in 1906 to the present time. The owners are hoping that one day Hardisty will have its own museum, at which time they plan to donate the memorabilia they have collected.

Antiques, collectibles, and crafts are accepted on consignment. They are for sale and are displayed throughout the house.

# LUND AND HAYS TEA ROOM

725 – 11 Avenue SE
High River, AB   T1V 1P6
(403) 652-5655

*Joyce Chrisp Watson, Karin and Lori Chrisp, Owners/Managers*

High River is located on Highway #2A, approximately 40 km south of Calgary.

The tea room is wheelchair accessible. Parking is available on site.

*HOURS:*　　　Monday through Saturday from
　　　　　　　9:30 a.m. to 4:30 p.m.
　　　　　　　7:00 p.m. to 10:00 p.m. for Just Desserts

*MENU:*

A choice of homemade soups, freshly baked bread, cinnamon buns, and homemade desserts are featured.

Beverages include cappuccino, espresso, latte, herbal teas, flavoured coffees, soft drinks, and fruit juices.

*DECOR:*

A handpainted floor and stencilled walls create a very homey and welcoming atmosphere. Artwork from local artists, hand-sewn crafts, antiques, plush animals, greeting cards, candles, and other crafts are for sale throughout the tea room.

Reflecting the building's overall theme of an old town, various rooms have old fashioned windows, doors and false fronts, and are furnished with antique furniture. Each room is a setting for dried flower arrangements and has a unique theme – such as the "Milliners Mercantile" room which recreates an old farmhouse kitchen, complete with wood stove. Window shopping is encouraged as you saunter down "main street."

*HISTORY:*

The tea room name combines the maiden names of Joyce's mother and mother-in-law, Gladys Lund and Carrie Hay.

Located in the front of the Garden Emporium in a renovated warehouse and former welding shop, the tea room opened in November 1995.

# *The Pic-A-Lilli Tea House and Crofters Cottage*

**Junction of Highway #14 and Secondary Road #855**
**Holden, AB   T0B 2C0**
**(403) 688-3636**

*Shelly and Trevor Fairbrother, Owners*

Located approximately 65 km southeast of Edmonton on Highway #14 at the Holden junction.

The tea house is wheelchair accessible. Ample parking is available.

*HOURS:*    Open daily from May 8 to December 22, please see the menu for further details.

Phone ahead to confirm hours.

*MENU:*

Continental breakfast is served daily between 9:30 a.m. and 10:30 a.m. Lunch is served Monday to Saturday between 11:30 a.m. and 1:30 p.m. Full course dinner specials, for which reservations are necessary, are served Monday to Saturday between 5:30 p.m. and 7:30 p.m., and Sunday between 11:30 a.m. and 2:00 p.m., and 5:00 p.m. and 7:30 p.m.

Tea, scones, and desserts are served anytime. Homemade specialties such as soups, breadbuns, sandwiches, salads, cinnamon buns, chocolate cheesecake, and a special Pic-A-Lilli relish are also available. Beverages include a variety of teas, coffees, and cold drinks.

*DECOR:*

The tea room is decorated in a country-kitchen theme with various paintings and crafts. The windows let in an abundance of natural light which accents the light-coloured walls.

The nearby Crofters Cottage contains many antiques, arts and crafts, paintings, ceramics, cross stitching, stained glass, woodworking items, and much more.

Wagon and sleigh rides can be arranged on request. Private functions may be booked between December and May. Please phone for further details.

*HISTORY:*

This converted farm house was completely renovated and first opened as a tea house in 1991.

The garden adjacent to the house offers a private hideaway of quiet green with a small pond. It was named by its previous owners after James Herriot's story, "Pic-A-Lilli Saves My Bacon." The tea house is a pleasant and enjoyable stop along the highway.

# KATY JANE'S TEA ROOM

5713 – 51 Avenue
Innisfail, AB   T4G 1R4
(403) 227-4881

**Operated by the Dr. George House Preservation Society**

Innisfail is located at the junction of Highways #2 and #2A, 26 km south of Red Deer.

The main floor is wheelchair accessible. Parking is available on the street.

*HOURS:*      Please phone for hours of operation.

*MENU:*

Features light lunches, delectable desserts, regular and specialty teas and coffees.


*DECOR:*

The main and second floors of the house, including the tea room area, have been restored to a 1920s style. Some original woodwork remains intact throughout the house, as well as some wainscotting on some of the walls on the second floor. The exterior of the building has been restored, and flower beds and a herb garden have been added.


*HISTORY:*

The tea room is located in the Dr. George residence, known locally as the Kemp house. In 1889, Dr. George and his family emigrated from England to Calgary, moving to Innisfail four years later. Constructed in 1893 on Quality Hill, the house has remained a landmark in the town.

Dr. and Mrs. George were both interested in natural history and established a museum in their home, the first in the then North West Territories. It was renamed the Innisfail Museum and later relocated in Red Deer when the family moved there in 1907. Mrs. George was an artist and is reputed to have designed the original provincial crest for Alberta and the official coat of arms for the City of Strathcona.

In 1907, the house was acquired by William and Katy Jane Kemp, early pioneers in the Innisfail district. Widowed in 1920, Katy supported herself and her sons by opening up the house for room and board. The house was subsequently rented until the 1960s. Designated a Provincial Historic Resource by Alberta Community Development in 1977, the house was later restored by the Dr. George House Preservation Society.

# Chateau Lake Louise

**Canadian Pacific Hotels Corporation
Lake Louise, AB   T0L 1E0
(403) 522-3511**

*Marlene Boone, Manager*

Located approximately 50 km northwest of Banff on Highway #1. Turn off at Lake Louise Village and follow the signs up to the lake.

The hotel is wheelchair accessible. A large parking lot is within walking distance.

*HOURS:*    Afternoon tea is served from May to September between the hours of 12:00 noon and 4:00 p.m.

*MENU:*

This four-course afternoon tea consists of two crumpets served with honey butter and fresh blueberries or other fruit in season, fruit compote in orange sauce, finger sandwiches with a variety of fillings, a choice of fancy pastries, and a pot of tea, at a cost of $13.95 per person.

*DECOR:*

Tea is served elegantly and leisurely in the main lobby of the hotel with superb views of the lake. Other restaurants within the hotel cater to a variety of tastes. This is a wonderful way to wind down and relax after a walk down to the end of the lake.

*HISTORY:*

Lake Louise was named after one of Queen Victoria's daughters. The Chateau Lake Louise is an historic landmark that has been a part of Lake Louise since 1890. It started out as a single level, wooden chalet on the shore of the emerald-coloured lake, and consisted of a sitting room, a kitchen, a bedroom, and a veranda. In 1892, the building inexplicably burned to the ground.

A second chalet was built in 1893 to accommodate about a dozen guests. At that time, there were no more than 100 guests during the summer, and visitors would camp along the lakeshore and visit the chalet for afternoon tea.

As the years passed, the number of visitors increased, and new wings were added to the existing buildings. A fire destroyed the wooden tudor-style structure in 1924, leaving the newer Painter wing unharmed. Canadian Pacific Railway built a new, eight-storey brick wing adjoining the Painter wing.

Extensively renovated in 1982, the hotel is now a year-round resort. The Glacier Wing was added in 1988, with further restorations in 1990. A new convention centre is currently under construction and is scheduled to open sometime in 1996.

# ENCHANTED COTTAGE TEASHOPPE

**Willow Lane**
**Highway #43**
**Little Smoky, AB   T0H 3Z0**
**(403) 524-2476**

*Shawnna Knight, Owner/Manager*

Located next to the river in the hamlet of Little Smoky, approximately 300 km northwest of Edmonton on Highway #43 (30 km southeast of Valleyview).

A small step into the building makes wheelchair assistance necessary. Ample parking is available in front of the building.

*HOURS:*        Tuesday to Saturday from 10:00 a.m. to 6:00 p.m.

Afternoon tea and specialty teas are served anytime and reservations are required. Specialty afternoon teas include:

Tea for Two – pot of tea with English biscuits . . . . . . . . . .$6.95 each

Cream Tea – pot of tea with scones, jam, and cream   . . . . .$4.95 each

Afternoon Tea – pot of tea, finger sandwiches,
one of either cake/biscuit, tart/biscuit, or two crumpets
w/butter and jam
(Cost of afternoon tea depends on
types of fillings requested.) . . . . . . . . . . . . . . . . . . . . . .$7.95 and up

Little Girls' Tea – pot of tea/juice served on china,
finger sandwiches, a fairy cake, biscuit, and a candy
to take home
(Cost of Little Girls' Tea depends on
types of fillings requested.) . . . . . . . . . . . . . . . . . . . . . .$4.95 and up

Victorian Tea – pot of tea, arrangement of either
cake and tarts or biscuits . . . . . . . . . . . . . . . . . . . . . . . . .$5.95 each

Scones and tea are served all day. A light menu is also available and includes home-style sandwiches, a ploughman's lunch, salad, and fresh desserts. All items are freshly made as ordered. There is a wide selection of teas, including loose, bagged, herbal and nonherbal, and specialty coffees are also available.

*DECOR:*

This newer barn building is set back from the highway and houses both the Teashoppe and gift shop which sells Victorian-style items, including potpourri, notepaper, old-fashioned-style cotton clothing, lace cloths, handmade crafts, jams, jellies, teas and tea accessories, and much more.

*HISTORY:*

The tea house is built on land that has been in the owner's family for three generations. This is a delightful spot set beside a busy highway and well worth the stop for a "cuppa."

# *Country At Heart*
# *Antiques and Tea House*

**Box 2141**
**44 Street and 47 Avenue**
**Lloydminster, SK   S9V 1R6**
**(306) 825-9498**

**Barb Gulka, Owner**

Located on the corner of 44 Street and 47 Avenue. Take Highway #16 East through Lloydminster to 47 Avenue. Tea House located just past 47 Avenue to the south.

The tea room is wheelchair accessible. Parking is available at the front of the house.

*Hours:*   Tea House is open from April 1 to December 31

April 1 to October 1 from 10:00 a.m. to 6:00 p.m.
October 2 to December 31 from 10:00 a.m. to 5:00 p.m.
Sunday from 1:00 p.m. to 5:00 p.m.
Closed Monday
Reservations appreciated

Small bread loaves (when available), scones, tea biscuits, muffins, cookies by the dozen, cinnamon buns, and pies (à la mode optional) are featured. Special desserts are displayed on a menu board. Lunch is served Tuesday to Friday from 11:30 a.m. to 2:00 p.m.

Beverages may be chosen from a variety of teas, coffees (regular, decaffeinated, and gourmet flavours), hot chocolate, iced tea, lemonade, and sugar-free fruit juice.

*DECOR:*

The tea room has a Victorian country motif. There are five theme rooms: the Linen and Lace room, Christmas room, Children's room, Country Kitchen and Pantry room, and Bath Product room. Antiques, musical bears, local arts and crafts, china, collectibles, dolls, gourmet foods, and other gift items are available for sale. Picnic tables are located outside and can be used by patrons, upon request.

The tea room is within walking distance of the museum grounds. Flower gardens and trees surround the tea house, making it a delightful stop for a break.

*HISTORY:*

This tea house is commonly referred to as the "Weaver Park House." It was built by Mr. Harvey Clayton Weaver in 1942. He was a modest and unassuming man with a love for soil and plants. He planted the grove of evergreen trees, fruit trees, and shrubs that surround the grounds. He was inducted into the Lloydminster Agricultural Hall of Fame in 1976, in recognition of his agricultural talents.

The Weaver House was rented out as a private residence by the city of Lloydminster until 1972. Twenty years later, in 1993, this landmark was converted into the present tea house. The present owners strive to maintain Mr. Weaver's philosophy and determination to "leave a place at least as good as, if not better, than when he found it."

# DAMON LANE'S TEA ROOM AND GIFT SHOP

**730 – 3rd Street SE**
**Medicine Hat, AB   T1A 0H7**
**(403) 529-2224**

*Joy and George Lukasiewich*
*Joy and Jody Lukasiewich, Tea Room Managers*

Located in Medicine Hat, 293 km southeast of Calgary on the Trans Canada Highway #1. From Highway #1, take lst street through the underpass, turn right onto Maple Avenue, then right onto 3rd Street.

The tea room is wheelchair accessible. Ample parking is available. The tea room has always been a smoke-free environment and is air-conditioned to ensure the comfort of guests in hot weather.

*HOURS:* Tuesday through Saturday from 10:00 a.m. to 5:00 p.m.

Tea and desserts served between 10:00 a.m. and 4:00 p.m.
Lunch served between 11:00 a.m. and 2:00 p.m.

*MENU:*

Everything is homemade. Old-time favourites are featured on the tea and dessert menu: scones, fruit crisps, lemon curd tarts, muffins, cookies, and squares. Beverages include specialty teas, coffee, hot chocolate, iced tea, and old-fashioned lemonade. The lunch menu includes soups, salads, cheese buns, bunwiches, and pitas. Special occasion celebrations can be accommodated. The guest book attests to visitors from all over the world, as well as memories from local guests.

*DECOR:*

The tea room is in the former living room of the house. The original woodwork, including a beamed ceiling in the living room, has never been painted and remains in very good condition. Windsor chairs and dark wood tables covered with white cloths create a cozy tea room atmosphere. They are further enhanced by the original wallpaper, a fireplace, original hardwood flooring, and a braided rug. Gift rooms are furnished with various antiques and collectibles, some of which are for sale.

*HISTORY:*

This charming bungalow is believed to have been built in 1912 by Ole Liens, who owned a lumber yard in Medicine Hat. Supposedly, whenever he found a piece of lumber he really liked, he brought it home to use in the building of the house. The house has had many other owners. The best known is Bob (Powder River) Smith who lived there for over thirty years with his wife, Belle, and their daughters. Everyone who knew him has a story to tell. Indeed, the house is best known locally as the Powder River Smith home.

There is another, more mysterious, occupant in the house. One rainy day a couple of years ago, an elderly man arrived on a motorcycle and said he had lived in the house as a teenager. He asked if anyone had ever seen a ghost there. He then told of a tall thin man in a dark suit who would get up from the sofa in the living room whenever anyone came to the door, walk into the centre of the room and then disappear. It was assumed he was waiting for someone special to come to the house. Although the owners have never seen Edgar, as they have affectionately named the ghost, he is blamed for unexplained occurrences!

# THE BOARDROOM TEA HOUSE

**Morinville Historical and Cultural Centre**
**10010 – 101 Street**
**Morinville, AB   T5R 1S1**
**(403) 939-2955**

*Darlene Belziuk, Manager*

Located north of Edmonton on Highway #2. Take Highway #2 north of St. Albert to Morinville. Exit at overpass to Morinville. Turn right at stop sign onto 101 Street and turn left on 100 Avenue.

The building is not wheelchair accessible. Parking is available at the back of the building.

*HOURS:*      Monday to Friday from 7:30 a.m. to 3:00 p.m.

*MENU:*

The menu features daily homemade lunch specials with a choice of two soups, two sandwich fillings, and pie for dessert. Cinnamon buns, toast, English muffins, variety muffins, caesar and tossed salads are also available. Beverages include regular and herbal teas, coffee, pop, juices, milk, homemade lemonade, and iced tea.

The Boardroom caters to small dinner parties, showers, anniversaries, and group bookings.

*DECOR:*

The tea room is the former boardroom of the old Convent Notre Dame de la Visitation and boarding school. The original shade of paint on the walls has been preserved from its earlier days. Dark wood window frames and doors, Tiffany lamp shades, dark green and floral-patterned linen, and balloon curtains add to the old-world atmosphere. Dried flower arrangements, antique oil lamps, old wringers, and milk churns are in keeping with the history of the building.

*HISTORY:*

The convent was built by the Filles de Jésus in 1909, with new additions built in 1920 and 1930. It served as a boarding school from approximately 1920 to 1965 for students from all over the province. Sold in 1968 to the Thibeault School District, it was then an elementary school for nine years. In 1977, it was acquired by the Morinville Historical and Cultural Society. On August 27, 1978, the building was declared a provincial historical resource by the government of Alberta. Photographs taken during the building's construction and subsequent additions, as well as class photos of staff and students, are located on the main hallway walls.

A museum is located on the main floor, and tours are available upon request.

# THE MCKEAGE HOUSE

**2202 – 21 Street**
**P.O. Box 1223**
**Nanton, AB   T0L 1R0**
**(403) 646-5724**

*Rita Green and Florence Brown, Owners*

Located one block south of Main Street (20 Street) on Highway #2 south.

Wheelchair accessibility is planned for 1996. There is ample parking available.

*HOURS:*        Open daily from 10:00 a.m. to 5:00 p.m.
                Open year-round

Items include homemade soups, sandwiches, and desserts. Special tea or coffee parties are arranged upon request. Evening or special occasion parties are also available as well as catering for special functions.

*DECOR:*

Crafts, collectibles, and antiques are displayed for sale throughout the house. Over 200 consignors have taken the opportunity to market their items here over the years.

*HISTORY:*

McKeage House was built before 1905 by Hamill. Between 1907 and 1910, the house was owned by A.J. Robertson, an MLA and leader of the Opposition Party in the first Alberta Legislature. It was purchased in 1910 by Dr. George Ernest McKeage who had his dental practice in the now-extended living room. Over the years, Dr. McKeage built additions onto the house as his son, daughter-in-law, and sister came to live with him. The house was sold in 1987 but kept the McKeage name.

# THE GINGER TEA ROOM AND GIFT SHOP

**43 Riverside Drive
P.O. Box 1230
Okotoks, AB   T0L 1T0
(403) 938-2907**

*Mernie and Rodney James, Owners*

Located south of Calgary on Highway #2. Turn west at the signs to Okotoks.

The tea room is wheelchair accessible. Ample parking is available.

*HOURS:*      Open daily from 10:00 a.m.
Last dinner reservation taken for 8:00 p.m.
Afternoon tea is served buffet-style between
2:30 p.m. and 4:00 p.m.

*MENU:*

Afternoon Tea:
>       mini-quiches with a variety of fillings, served in a chafing dish
>       an assortment of finger sandwiches
>       cakes
>       a pot of tea served with a tea cosy
>       $9.95 per person

Other house specialties:
>       Jumbo shrimp, chicken Parmesan, Rodney's favourite, stuffed
>       New York steak and prime rib.

A romantic dinner for two – $49.95
>       Chateaubriand, Arctic scampi, and a banana flambé.

The tea room also caters to group gatherings.


*DECOR:*

The tea room and gift shop are situated in a newly built (1990) Victorian-style stately mansion, complete with turreted rooms and a covered verandah. The tea room retains an old-world charm, decorated with chintz-style table linens. The walls are covered with an extensive selection of collector plates and shelves are filled with ornate pieces of china and pictures. The lawn, shrubs, and flower beds add a colourful approach to the verandah and front entrance of the building.

The Ginger Tea Room is listed in international publications and enjoys clientele from all over the world.

Collector plates, glassware, hand-crafted goods, clothing, chinaware, giftware, original paintings, and prints are for sale in the gift shop.


*HISTORY:*

In 1985, Mernie James opened The Ginger Room across the road from the present site. An additional 1200 square-foot expansion did little to alleviate the long wait for a table in the tea room. A new 6,500 square-foot mansion was built and opened its stained-glass doors in 1990. The owners hope that in ninety-nine years the building will have become the heritage site so many people already believe it to be.

# HERITAGE MANOR TEA HOUSE, BED AND BREAKFAST

**#1, 5401 – 49 Avenue**
**Olds, AB   T4H 1G3**
**(403) 556-6766**

*Miriam and Bill March, Hosts*

From Highway #2 south from Edmonton, exit at Highway #27 to Olds. Turn left onto 49 Avenue. Heritage Manor located at the end of 49 Avenue.

The house is wheelchair accessible. Ample parking is available. Heritage Manor is within walking distance of most amenities.

*HOURS:*    Tuesday to Saturday from 11:30 a.m. to 4:30 p.m.
Thursday and Friday from 7:00 p.m. to 9:00 p.m.
Closed Sunday and Monday

*MENU:*

Lunch: soup of the day served with a roll, fresh fruit, or a vegetable plate; also warm scones with jam, carrot cake, assorted pies, hot apple pie with rum sauce, ice cream, and butter tarts. Beverages include coffee (regular and flavoured), tea (small and large pots available), iced tea, juice, milk, and pop. Thursday and Friday evenings offer cappuccino, espresso, and cheesecake. Small groups or receptions can also be accommodated.

*DECOR:*

The house is decorated with restored antiques, including the tables and chairs in the tea room. It is situated on a large, beautifully landscaped lot. Four of the upstairs bedrooms are available for Bed and Breakfast.

*HISTORY:*

The house was built in 1898 by Fred Shackleton, a prominent area businessman, for his wife and seven children. Totally rebuilt in 1928, it was the first house in Olds to have electricity. The home has served the community in many ways, including as the Sherwood Home for the Aged, a boarding house, and a doctor's office.

Bill and Miriam March, the present owners, purchased the house in 1988.

# HONEYSUCKLE ROSE TEA HOUSE

**4903 – 49 Avenue**
**Onoway, AB   T0E 1V0**
**(403) 967-2727**

*Alvina Spreen, Owner*

Located northwest of Edmonton in the town of Onoway on Highway #43. From Edmonton take Highway #16 west. Exit north onto Highway #43. Exit into Onoway and follow Lac Ste Anne Street to 49 Street. Turn right, and go to 49 Avenue.

The tea house is not wheelchair accessible. Parking is available on the street and at the back of the building.

*Hours:*     Monday, Tuesday, and Thursday from
9:00 a.m. to 4:00 p.m.
Friday from 9:00 a.m. to 8:00 p.m.
Saturday from 10:30 a.m. to 4:00 p.m.
Sunday from 11:00 a.m. to 2:30 p.m.
Closed Wednesday
Phone ahead for hours. Reservations accepted.

Morning treats include raisin or cheese scones, cinnamon buns, and toast. Soups, sandwiches, croissants, and specialty desserts are available for lunch. Supper is served Friday evenings and the main course varies each week. Catering is available for small receptions.

*DECOR:*

The tea house is decorated in 1950s country style, with forest green and light blue wallpaper complementing green and blue tablecloths and tablemats. Scatter rugs cover a natural wood floor. Antiques, collectibles, handcrafted items, dried flower arrangements, and carved wood items are available for sale and displayed throughout the tea house.

*HISTORY:*

Built in 1938, the house was used as a private residence for many years. Unused and empty for some time, it opened as a tea house in December 1994. The current owners took over in April 1996.

# THE CRONQUIST HOUSE
# CRONQUIST HERITAGE CENTRE

**Box 224, Bower Ponds**
**Red Deer, AB   T4N 5E8**
**(403) 346-0055**

*Anne Michaels, Catering Manager*

Located south of Edmonton on Highway #2 in the city of Red Deer.

Coming from the north: take 67 Street exit into Red Deer to Taylor Drive. Turn south (right) onto Taylor Drive and follow it to Carry Wood Drive. Turn right onto Carry Wood Drive and follow the signs.

Coming from the south: take 32 Street exit into Red Deer to Taylor Drive. Turn north (left) onto Taylor and follow it to Carry Wood Drive. Turn left onto Carry Wood and follow the signs.

The tea room is wheelchair accessible. There is ample parking at the back of the house.

*HOURS:*    Monday to Friday from 9:00 a.m. to 4:00 p.m.
Sunday from 1:00 p.m. to 4:00 p.m.
The house is closed most Saturdays for private bookings.

*MENU:*

Afternoon tea is made to order and served daily. Scones with cream and jam are also available for $1.75. The lunch menu features soup, sandwiches, salads, and a daily special entrée. Coffee cake, chocolate cake, muffins, rhubarb crisp with ice cream, and a daily special dessert are also offered. Prices range from $1.95 for soup to $4.25 for vegetarian chili with corn bread. Daily special prices vary.

Beverages include regular and herbal teas, coffee, soft drinks, hot apple cider, milk, juice, and their own special blend of iced tea.

Catering services providing a variety of lunch, dinner, and finger-food items are available for a private party or office functions. Selections can be adjusted to suit dietary needs.

*DECOR:*

Two gift shops on the upper floor of the house offer assorted antiques, collectibles, and gift items. Special events are often scheduled for Sunday afternoons. Please phone for more information.

The Cronquist House is situated on the picturesque shore of Bower Ponds, a waterfowl sanctuary and tranquil spot amid city limits.

*HISTORY:*

Dating from the early 1900s, Cronquist House is one of the few remaining buildings in Red Deer from the time the area was first settled. The three-storey farm house was built in 1911 in Red Deer's West Park district. The original location fronted the old Calgary-Edmonton Trail with a wonderful view of the Red Deer River valley. The owners believe Cronquist House to be the first tea house in Central Alberta. The house was moved to its present site at Bower Ponds and restored by the Red Deer International Folk Festival Society in 1976. It was designated a Municipal Historic Resource in August 1982.

# *That's Crafty!*

**Highway #9, West of Drumheller**
**Rosebud, AB   T0J 2T0**
**(403) 677-2207**

*June Evans, Owner/Manager*

Located 26 km west of Drumheller on Highway #9, one hour northeast of Calgary.

Both the barn and the tea room are wheelchair accessible. Ample parking is available near the barn with a large circular drive which permits easy movement for buses and motorhomes.

*Hours:*    Open from mid-March until Christmas
Monday to Saturday from 10:00 a.m. to 5:00 p.m.
Closed Sunday

All items on the menu are homemade and include soups, salads, and vegetable plates. The dessert choices feature carrot cake, chocolate fudge cake with hot caramel sauce, various cheesecakes, giant cinnamon buns, and muffins.

Specialty teas are served in porcelain tea pots and collectible tea cups and saucers. Coffee is served in "cowboy" cups. Juices, pop, and mineral water are also available.

## *DECOR:*

The tea room is located in an old dairy barn seating about 50 people. The view from the tea room stretches across miles of rolling prairie and farm land. A large deck provides outdoor seating during the summer months.

Each year the decor is changed to provide a new theme. This year's motif is western with barn wood, wheat crafts, antiques, and collectibles filling the tea room. It features work from over 250 artisans.

## *HISTORY:*

That's Crafty! is a tea room and craft barn housed in a 1940's dairy barn. It was converted in 1992 to the present tea room.

# MAXINE'S CAFÉ

**29 Perron Street**
**St. Albert, AB   T8N 1E6**
**(403) 460-1699**

*Ann MacDonell, Manager*

Located in downtown St. Albert. From Edmonton, take Highway #2 north to St. Albert. Turn left onto St. Anne Street. Turn right onto Perron Street. The Café is a half block down on the right hand side.

Maxine's is wheelchair accessible. Parking is available on Perron Street.

*HOURS:* Tuesday, Wednesday, Thursday, and Sunday from 11:30 a.m. to 3:00 p.m. and 5:00 p.m. to 9:00 p.m.

Friday and Saturday from 11:30 a.m. to 3:00 p.m. and 5:00 p.m. to 10:00 p.m.

Afternoon Tea is served daily from 2:00 p.m. to 4:00 p.m. Sunday Brunch is served from 10:30 a.m. to 2:30 p.m. Closed Monday and daily from 3:00 p.m. to 5:00 p.m. (except if Afternoon Tea is ordered)

Afternoon tea includes assorted sandwiches, scones, fancy cakes, and petits fours, served on a three-tiered china plate. The cost is $9.95 per person and reservations are required.

Daily lunch and dinner specials are available on the regular menu. Lunch items include soup, quiche, pasta, chicken, and salad as well as scones, appetizers, and a selection of cakes and tortes for dessert. Dinner choices vary daily and feature specialty chicken, meat, and fish dishes. All dishes are gourmet fare and are made from fresh ingredients. An extensive selection of teas includes regular and herbal varieties, coffees, as well as espresso and caffè latte.

*DECOR:*

The café is decorated in a floral motif with various bric-à-brac, dried flowers, photographs, and pictures. Seasonal themes are evident throughout the year.

*HISTORY:*

Maxine's was opened in March 1992 by Ron Swist and his wife, Maxine. The café was modelled after several west coast tea houses including one of Maxine's favourites, "The Blethering Place" at Oak Bay in Victoria, B.C. After Maxine's death, her husband, Ron, with the help of friends, relatives, employees, and restaurant manager Ann MacDonell, continued running the café. It is now one of the most popular restaurants in St. Albert. With the addition of chef Ajay Lala, Maxine's was awarded the Edmonton Journal's "Golden Plate Award" for 1995.

Located in downtown St. Albert adjacent to the Sturgeon River, Maxine's is within walking distance to riverside walking trails for a leisurely stroll before or after your visit.

# McDonald House of Treasures

**4918 – 47 Street**
**Box 247**
**Sedgewick, AB   T0B 4C0**
**(403) 384-2467**

*John and Karen Wold, Owners*

Located on Highway #13, one hour east of Camrose. The tea house is located at the end of Main Street in Sedgewick, beside the town park.

The tea house is wheelchair accessible from the back door. Parking is available on the street or across the back alley.

*Hours:*   Open Monday to Friday only from 10:00 a.m. to 5:00 p.m.
Open weekends June to August
Open by appointment anytime

*MENU:*

A variety of coffees and teas, iced tea in the summer, and homemade desserts are featured. Light lunches are available upon request (please call ahead). The tea room is available for birthday parties, meetings, etc., and has seating capacity for up to 12 people.

*DECOR:*

Surrounded by tall old trees, lawns, and flowers, the house is decorated in a country style with antiques, collectibles, and crafts which are for sale. A wood heater adds extra coziness on winter days.

*HISTORY:*

This two-storey home was built around 1907 by J.S. McDonald. It has also served as a courtroom, a doctor's office, and a boarding house.

# THE VICTORIAN TEA HOUSE

**Golden Spike Road**
**Box 3642**
**Spruce Grove, AB   T7X 3A2**
**(403) 962-3177**

*Kaye and Duncan Oliver, Gary and Lynn Dika, Owners/Managers*

Located southwest of Edmonton. Take Highway #16X west to Spruce Grove. Turn south at first exit to Spruce Grove. Follow road south until it becomes Golden Spike Road. The tea house is located 1 mile south of Highway #16 on Golden Spike Road.

The tea house is wheelchair accessible. There is ample parking.

*Hours:*   Wednesday to Sunday, 11:00 a.m. to 9:00 p.m.
Closed Monday and Tuesday
Afternoon Tea is served between
2:00 p.m. and 4:00 p.m.

*MENU:*

Afternoon Tea: a variety of dainty sandwiches, cakes
freshly baked scones with Devonshire cream
tea or coffee
$9.95 per person

Lunch: soups, salads, sandwiches, entrées

Dinner: chicken, beef, and seafood specialties prepared in a traditional English style

Beverages: a wide variety of teas, coffee, juice, and milk

There are separate menus for Sunday brunch, lunch, and dinner.


*DECOR:*

The atmosphere is relaxed with soothing background music. Service is not rushed, so it is better not to be in a hurry. Enjoy and relax!

Meals are served in three areas of the main floor: the former living room, the dining room, and the veranda. The interior is attractively decorated with floral wallpaper and curtains paired with dark oak accents. Wall decor includes antiques, framed country scenes, and floral arrangements. A brick fireplace in the living room area enhances the cozy atmosphere. All wall and window coverings are replica patterns from the Victoria & Albert Museum in London, England. The waitresses are dressed in ankle-length, black dresses with white aprons.

The four bedrooms are now part of a gift shop, each having a different theme: scented candles/potpourri, toys, teas and jams, and soaps. A large variety of teas, linens and laces, handcrafted jewellery, unique giftwares, and gift certificates complete the list of items available. All is very pleasing to the eye and nose!


*HISTORY:*

Originally a farm and family home, the house was built in 1913 by Austrian pioneer Philip Schultz and his wife, Christina. The Schultzs and their seventeen children were one of the founding families of the Spruce Grove area.

# THE BELL'S TEA HOUSE

**4720 – 49 Street
Box 1291
Stettler, AB   T0C 2L0
(403) 742-3242**

*Iain and Val Bell, Owners*

Located on 49 Street. Take 50 Street (Main Street) to 48 Avenue, turn east, follow 48 Avenue to 49 Street.

Assistance with wheelchairs is available. Ample street parking is available, as well as parking at the rear of the tea house.

*Hours:*     Monday to Friday from 10:00 a.m. to 5:00 p.m.
Saturday from 11:00 a.m. to 4:00 p.m
Closed Sunday and public holidays

*MENU:*

Afternoon Tea:  $14.95 for two (24-hour notice required)
a selection of dainty sandwiches and sweets

Cream Teas:  $1.50 per person
scone with jam and Devonshire cream

Lunches:  choice of two home-cooked soups served in a mini-loaf, salads, sandwiches, crab melt, lasagna, grilled sole, and a ploughman's lunch; rich cakes and light desserts

Beverages:  regular, specialty, and decaffeinated teas, coffee, milk, orange juice, flavoured hot chocolate, and assorted fruit drinks

*DECOR:*

The tea house is decorated in a Victorian theme with floral wallpaper and paintings.

A Gift Shoppe is also situated in the house featuring many items such as artwork, needle crafts, framed prints, Victorian stationery, quilts, stained glass, pottery, woodcarvings, and collectibles.

*HISTORY:*

The house was built in 1905 by Mr. George R. Farmer, who owned the first hardware store in Stettler. Later, it was the Presbyterian Manse for many years. In the early 1920s, it became the Mill's Hospital supervised by Dr. (Col.) Archie Kennedy and is believed to be one of the first hospitals to serve Stettler and the surrounding rural area. In the late 1930s, the house became a private dwelling once again. Iain and Val Bell bought and moved into the house in 1993. After many months of interior renovation, the tea house opened in February 1994.

# COUNTRY LACE COTTAGE TEA HOUSE AND GIFT SHOP

4805 – 52 Avenue
Stony Plain, AB   T7Z 1C4
(403) 968-2222

*Leanne Weatherald and Marijke Barter, Owners/Managers*

Located in the town of Stony Plain. Take Highway #16 or #16X and exit at Stony Plain. Go south to third traffic light (52 Avenue), turn right. Tea house is on the right-hand side.

The Cottage is wheelchair accessible, although the upper loft is not. Parking is available on the street.

*HOURS:*    Monday, Tuesday, Wednesday, and Saturday from
8:00 a.m. to 5:00 p.m.
Thursday and Friday from 8:00 a.m. to 9:00 p.m.
Sunday and holidays from 11:00 a.m. to 3:00 p.m.

Afternoon tea is served between 2:00 p.m. and 4:00 p.m.

*MENU:*

Afternoon tea is served on a three-tiered china plate, with tea or coffee, at a cost of $6.95 per person and features an assortment of finger sandwiches, scones, and cakes:

*Maids of Honour:*    A rich cake with a puff pastry base, filled with a flavoured curd

*Eccles Cake:*    A rich puff pastry cake, stuffed with currants

*Sally Lunn Tea Cakes:*    A very light cake made as large buns, split and served with thick clotted cream

*Scones:*    Oven baked, cut into wedges, and served with preserves and butter

Other menu items include fresh muffins, cinnamon buns, cookies, cheesecake, and pies. Specialty desserts are available daily. Light lunches feature soup, salads, sandwiches, and quiche. Flavored teas, coffees, hot chocolate, iced tea, juices, and flavoured spring water complete the menu.

*DECOR:*

This nonsmoking tea house has a warm, country atmosphere with a dark green and cream motif, and a collection of various pine tables and chairs. Numerous windows and a vaulted ceiling create a light and airy setting. There is a games table in front of the fireplace where you can challenge your friends. An upper loft features local crafts as well as a place to curl up and relax with a "cuppa" and a good book.

*HISTORY:*

The tea house is located on a street where several older homes have been converted into new businesses. The Country Lace Cottage is a new building with an old-fashioned look situated on a large, mature lot.

# THE HOMESTEADER'S KITCHEN

**Stony Plain Multicultural Heritage Centre**
**5411 – 51 Street**
**Stony Plain, AB   T7Z 1X7**
**(403) 963-2777**

*Darlene Lealand, Manager*

Located 20 minutes west of Edmonton on Highways #16 and #16X in the town of Stony Plain. Take either Highway #16 or #16X to the Stony Plain overpass. Travel south to 53 Avenue and turn right. Turn left at 51 Street and follow the road to the centre.

The centre is not wheelchair accessible. Street parking is available. Donation requested upon entering.

*HOURS:*    Monday to Saturday from 11:30 a.m. to 3:00 p.m. for full meal service
From 3:00 p.m. to 4:00 p.m. for pie and coffee

Sunday from 11:30 a.m. to 6:30 p.m. for full meal service

*MENU:*

Daily specials include homemade soup, salads, quiche, and sandwiches; the homesteader's stew is just right for those hearty appetites! Homebaked bread is served with every meal. The dessert trolley offers a selection of up to eight kinds of homemade pie. Coffee, tea, hot chocolate, pop, lemonade, juices, iced tea, and milk are also available. A children's menu includes grilled cheese sandwiches, a small beverage, and ice cream.

Take-out items such as loaves of bread, buns, perogies, cabbage rolls, quiche, and pie are available with 24-hour notice.

Every Friday is Ukrainian Day and homemade perogies, cabbage rolls, and kubasa are featured. An English roast beef dinner with Yorkshire pudding is a Sunday specialty.


*DECOR:*

Meals are served in two rooms on the lower floor: the Homesteader's Kitchen, decorated in a country theme with wooden tables and chairs, and the Gallery Restaurant, displaying the work of local artists. Waitresses in long dresses and period aprons enhance the old-world charm.


*HISTORY:*

Built in 1925, the building was the first high school in the Stony Plain region until 1949, after which it fell into disrepair and was slated for demolition. The Heritage Agricultural Society leased "the brick school-house" in 1974, and after extensive restoration and renovation it opened as the Multicultural Heritage Centre. Now designated an historic site, many photographs and artifacts documenting the history of the area are displayed throughout the building. On the first floor, the Settler's Cabin is a living museum. Craft shops sell the work of local and international artisans.

A stroll through the lovely award-winning grounds along paths and past fountain ponds, lawns, and old shade trees is a pleasant beginning or conclusion to a visit to the Centre. The Opperthauser House, the Historical Library and Archives for the region, and a public art gallery are also located within the grounds.

# THE HIDING PLACE TEA ROOM

**206 Centre Street N
Sundre, AB   T0M 1X0
(403) 638-3431**

*Helen and Trevor Morgan, Owners*

Located on Highway #27, 40 km west of Olds, and one block north of the four-way stop after entering Sundre.

The tea room is wheelchair accessible. Street parking is available.

*HOURS:*      Monday to Saturday from 10:00 a.m. to 4.30 p.m., year-round
Closed Sunday and statutory holidays

*MENU:*

Includes soups, a variety of sandwiches, daily dinner specials, salads, muffins, sweet dough buns, carrot cake, ice cream and flaky pastry fruit pies. A children's menu is available. Beverages offered are coffee, regular and herbal teas, hot apple cider, hot chocolate, soft drinks, fruit juices, sparkling water, milk, and chocolate milk.

*DECOR:*

The tea room's furnishings provide a peaceful and relaxing atmosphere. A book store attached to the tea room expresses Helen's life-long love of books.

*HISTORY:*

Helen Morgan grew up on a farm west of Olds, Alberta. Her parents' home was a frequent stopping place for settlers and ranchers who were always welcomed with a meal. Opening a tea room was Helen's dream. Continuing the tradition of her parents, she visualized a place with a restful, gracious, caring atmosphere where people who were tired and stressed could come as a peaceful pause in their journey.

The tea room opened in May 1994 and its name comes from Psalm 37.

# St. Ann Ranch Trading Co.

P.O. Box 249
Highway 21
Trochu, AB   T0M 2C0
(403) 442-3924

*Lewis, Lorene and Louis Frere, Proprietors*

Located approximately 110 km southeast of Red Deer. Take Highway #595 east out of Red Deer. Turn south onto Highway #21. Follow it to Trochu, turn east into Trochu and follow the signs.

The tea room has a small entrance step which may be difficult for wheelchairs; a patio is open for outside seating. Ample parking is available.

*HOURS:*    Tuesday to Saturday from 1:00 p.m. to 5:00 p.m.
May 1 to September 30

Includes home-baked Saskatoon and rhubarb desserts, biscuits, cinnamon buns, carrot cake, croissants with homemade jams, and an occasional "special of the day." Cold beverages, teas, coffee, cappuccino, hot apple cider, and hot chocolate are also available. Meals are served on elegant, antique china, in keeping with the historic character of the old house. The tea house also caters to seniors and other groups; special lunch and dinner parties for large groups are available by reservation only.

*DECOR:*

Located in the walk-out basement of the house, the tea room is furnished faithfully to the early settlement theme. Old wood panelling, green table linens, and white lace cloths create a cozy atmosphere. Shelves hold antique crockery, tea pots, glass and granite ware, primitives, books, linens, furniture, and jewellery – all for sale.

*HISTORY:*

This four-storey, 30-room house is the original St. Ann Ranch Trading Co., established in 1905 by a group of aristocratic cavalrymen from Brittany, France. A major French settlement soon developed, continuing homeland customs. Other groups followed, including the Fathers of Tinchebray in 1905, The North West Mounted Police in 1907, and the Sisters of Charity d'Evron, France in 1909. By the time World War I broke out, the community was thriving. The cavalrymen all returned to defend their homeland; only five returned.

The ranch site is now operated as a farm by a descendent of one of the original families. Rooms in the upper floors of the house are available for bed and breakfast; an adjacent 1904 cabin offers the opportunity to experience early pioneer life.

The original townsite is being recreated near the main house. Eight historic buildings are now museums and an interpretive centre displays an extensive collection of early photographs, letters, and diaries. Tours are also available. When Trochu recently celebrated its ninetieth anniversary, it was attended by over 50 descendants of the original French settlers.

# VALLEY ROSE TEA ROOM

**146 Main Street
Turner Valley, AB   T0L 2A0
(403) 933-2972**

*Roberta Kerr, Proprietor*

Located 45 minutes south of Calgary on Highway #22.

The tea room is wheelchair accessible. Parking is available in an adjacent parking lot.

*Hours:*     *Summer:* Daily from 7:00 a.m. to 8:00 p.m.

*Winter:*   Monday to Friday from
11:00 a.m. to 3:00 p.m.
Saturday and Sunday from
10:00 a.m. to 3:00 p.m.

*MENU:*

A Country Tea of tea, hot homemade biscuits, jam, and a special cream is available for $4.50 per person. Breakfast is served all day and features eggs, omelettes, pancakes, French toast, and toast and jam. Home baking includes muffins, cakes, and pies. Weekend brunch consists of eggs benedict with crabmeat or ham and Swiss cheese on homemade biscuits. Light lunches of soup, salads, and sandwiches are also available. Daily specials are posted on the sandwich board. Home-cooked, grandma-style dinners with chicken and dumplings, Swiss steak, roast pork, beef, or chicken are served. Reservations are recommended.

*DECOR:*

Large windows let in an abundance of sunshine, and the pink and peach colour scheme give the tea room an ambiance just like Grandma's home. Patrons are welcome to sit outside in the wildflower garden during the summer months.

*HISTORY:*

The building has had many uses and locations throughout its history. Built in the 1930s during the oil boom, it has been a Chinese laundry in Longview, a restaurant in Millarville, and the municipal district office in Turner Valley. An interesting feature of the tea room is a vault the size of a walk-in closet located in the back wall. Installed in 1944 when the building was moved to Turner Valley, two failed robbery attempts proved the vault's security. The tumblers on the vault were removed in 1954 when the building became an insurance agency.

On the grounds is a typical "shack" in which men, and sometimes families, lived in the 1920s and 1930s during the oil boom era.

# THE FAMILY TREE TEA HOUSE

**9828 – 106 Street**
**Westlock, AB   T0G 2L0**
**(403) 349-5030**

*Roxanne Mutch and Jeff Kalmbach, Owners*

Located 85 km north of Edmonton. Take Highway #2 north to Westlock, turn west at Highway #18, and follow highway for 10 km to Westlock.

The tea house is not wheelchair accessible. Ample parking is available on the street.

*HOURS:*       Monday to Saturday from 10:00 a.m. to 5:00 p.m.
Closed Sunday

*MENU:*

Light lunches consist of homemade soup and/or sandwiches made with freshly baked croissants, as well as cheesecake, tortes, muffins, and fresh cinnamon buns. A large variety of beverages are served: regular, herbal and iced teas, regular and specialty coffees, espressos, lattes, and cappuccinos; floats, juices, pop, and milk.

Seating for 21 people is available in the living room and dining room; tables are placed on the front veranda during the summer months.


*DECOR:*

The tea house has three rooms, a kitchen, a bedroom and a living room, all of which are decorated in a country style. The main floor living room has a Victorian theme. Crafts from local artisans, including dried flower arrangements, wood furniture, shelving, antiques, collectibles, and tole painted wall hangings, are displayed and available for sale.

A custom picture-framing business is located in the second, main floor bedroom.


*HISTORY:*

The house was built in the late 1920s and is a tribute to the fine workmanship and design of the era. Its gleaming white paint and the huge lathe-turned pillars supporting the front porch roof made this house stand out from those around it. Equal care and attention was given to the interior of the house, with finely crafted mouldings accentuating the beauty of the hardwood floors. All of this conveys a warm and inviting feeling.

# MacEachern Tea House and Restaurant

**4719 – 50 Avenue**
**Wetaskiwin, AB   T9A OR9**
**(403) 352-8308**

*Wendy McFaul, Owner/Manager*

Located approximately 110 km south of Edmonton on Highway #2. Turn east at Highway #13 to Wetaskiwin.

The MacEachern Tea House is not wheelchair accessible. Ample parking is available in front of and behind the house.

**HOURS:**   *Summer:*   Open 7 days a week from 9:30 a.m to
4:30 p.m. from the May long weekend to
September long weekend
Reservations recommended between
11:30 a.m. and 1:30 p.m.

*Winter:*   Monday to Saturday from
9:30 a.m. to 4:00 p.m.

Afternoon tea is served anytime during the afternoon.

*MENU:*

Afternoon Tea:     Traditional fresh scones with preserves
                   Devonshire cream or butter
                   $2.95 each or $5.25 for two

A choice of over 20 teas includes Darjeeling, Earl Grey, English Breakfast, orange pekoe, decaffeinated blackcurrant, specialty, and herbal teas. Tea pots come with cosies; loose tea is served with strainers. A large selection of espresso and specialty coffees are also available.

Daily specials, as well as homemade soups and chowders, salads, bagels, cheesecakes, and other desserts complete the menu. The house caters to special occasions such as breakfast meetings, business lunches, and small receptions by appointment only.

*DECOR:*

The interior decor is Edwardian-style with beamed ceilings and racks for china and bric-à-brac.

The Kitchen Cupboard on the upper floor specializes in various kitchen utensils, crockery, china, books, and glassware.

*HISTORY:*

Built in 1903, the house was owned by the Duncan MacEachern family until the early 1950s. Duncan MacEachern, an early pioneer and mayor of Wetaskiwin, established a flour mill which continued operating until the 1960s.

# RITA'S BOUTIQUE AND TEA HOUSE

**Box 85**
**Widewater, AB   T0G 2M0**
**(403) 369-3743**

*Rita Brisebois and Marie Butz, Owners/Managers*

Located in the town of Widewater, 10 minutes northwest of Slave Lake, on Highway #2.

The tea house is not wheelchair accessible. Parking is available alongside the building.

*HOURS:*  Thursday and Friday from 10:30 a.m. to 4:00 p.m.
Saturday from 10:30 a.m. to 5:00 p.m.
Sunday from 1:00 p.m. to 5:00 p.m.

Homemade soups, deli sandwiches, scrumptious desserts, and specialty coffees and teas are offered.


*DECOR:*

The tea house is located in a beautiful setting in Slave Lake country. It specializes in antiques, country wood crafts, Victorian gifts, and much more. All are available for sale in the tea room.

# *"Tea Leaves"*

We would like to leave you with a short selection of books and a calendar we have gathered about afternoon tea. All contain recipes, many give the history of tea and tea making, and others include menus and mail-order tea merchant information.


Foley, Tricia, *Having Tea – Recipes and Table Settings*, written by Catherine Calvert, photographs by Keith Scott Morton (New York, N.Y.: Clarkson N. Potter, Inc., 1987)

Mackley, Leslie, *The Book of Afternoon Tea*, (Los Angeles: HP Books, a division of Price Stern Sloan; published by arrangement with Salamander Books Ltd., 1992)

Miller, Joni, with photographs by Martin Brigdale, *The Collectible Teapot and Tea Calendar for 1996* (New York: Workman Publishing, published simultaneously in Canada by Thomas Allen and Son Limited, 1995)

Tovey, John, *Afternoon Teas*, A Sainsbury Cookbook (Cambridge, U.K.: Martin Books, Simon & Schuster Consumer Group, 1992)

Trygg, Koren and Lucy Poshek, *Afternoon Tea* (Yellow Springs, Ohio: an Antioch Gourmet Gift Book, Antioch Publishing Co., 1992)

*Victoria – The Charms of Tea: Reminiscences and Recipes* (New York, N.Y.: Hearst Books, an affiliate of William Morrow & Company, Inc., 1991)

Wrightman, Yvonne, *All the Tea in China* (Regina, Sask.: Centax Books, 1994)

If you would like to receive more copies of *Time for Tea*, please complete the form below:

Name: _______________________________________________

Address: _____________________________________________

_____________________________________________

Postal Code: _________________________________________


Number of Copies Requested: ____________

Cost per book: $12.95

Total Cost of Book(s): ____________

Postage and handling: $3.50 per book

Subtotal: ____________

GST 7% of Subtotal: ____________

Total Order: ____________

Enclosed is a: ☐ Cheque ☐ Money Order


Please make cheques and money orders payable to **Time for Tea**. **Allow 4-6 weeks for delivery.** No C.O.D. orders


Mail order to: **Time for Tea**
P.O. Box 77014
Grandin Park Post Office
St. Albert, AB Canada  T8N 6C1

If you would like to receive more copies of *Time for Tea*, please complete the form below:

Name: _______________________________________________

Address: _____________________________________________

_____________________________________________

Postal Code: _________________________________________


Number of Copies Requested: _______________

Cost per book: $12.95

Total Cost of Book(s): _______________

Postage and handling: $3.50 per book

Subtotal: _______________

GST 7% of Subtotal: _______________

Total Order: _______________


Enclosed is a: ☐ Cheque ☐ Money Order


Please make cheques and money orders payable to **Time for Tea**.
**Allow 4-6 weeks for delivery.**
No C.O.D. orders


Mail order to: **Time for Tea**
P.O. Box 77014
Grandin Park Post Office
St. Albert, AB Canada  T8N 6C1